Words of Freedom
THE U.S. CONSTITUTION

by Kristin Cashore

Editorial Offices: Glenview, Illinois • Parsippany, New Jersey • New York, New York

Sales Offices: Needham, Massachusetts • Duluth, Georgia • Glenview, Illinois
Coppell, Texas • Sacramento, California • Mesa, Arizona

The United States Constitution

In 1783 the American Revolution came to an end. However, the end of the war did not bring an end to the troubles that the young nation faced.

In 1781 the Continental Congress wrote the Articles of Confederation. With the Articles, American leaders established a weak central government with one branch—Congress. They remembered what it was like to suffer under British rule. They did not want America's central government to be strong and tyrannous, like Britain's was.

The powers of Congress were so limited that, for example, it could not tax the people. This meant that Congress had little money to run the country. It also could not make trade laws with other nations. Therefore, the United States was unable to create strong trade relations with other nations. Because of the weak central government, our nation was neither stable nor strong.

Many of our nation's early leaders met at the Constitutional Convention in 1787.

When the **delegates** to the Constitutional Convention met in Philadelphia in 1787, they knew that the United States needed a more effective government. Some wanted the government to be strong so that the country would be stable. Others wanted the government to be weak to protect the rights of the people.

After a lot of debate and many **compromises**, the delegates wrote the United States Constitution. The Constitution created a strong central government with three branches: the **legislative branch**, the **executive branch**, and the **judicial branch**. The Constitution, however, also protected the people by creating **checks and balances** and leaving many powers to the states. It was also decided that the Constitution could also be amended.

The people who wrote the Constitution did not always agree, but in their wisdom, they came together and cooperated. Each person's contribution was important.

George Washington: The Leader of the Constitutional Convention

The delegates to the Constitutional Convention were lawyers, soldiers, businesspeople, and merchants. More than half of the delegates had fought in the Revolutionary War, and many had helped write their states' constitutions. But even among these distinguished people, one stood out as a leader: George Washington.

Washington was a popular man. Against all odds, he had led the American troops to victory in the Revolutionary War. Many admired and respected him. Washington was a true American Patriot. He did not want personal power. He wanted what was best for the people. Washington put his own glory aside and worked instead for the good of the country and its citizens.

George Washington wanted what was best for the people, not what was best for himself.

George Washington was admired by many during the Revolutionary War.

Washington was one of the people who called for the Constitutional Convention. He could see that the government of the United States was not effective. Washington knew that the states would not work well together unless the central government was made stronger. He favored a new Constitution and a more powerful national government.

The delegates unanimously elected Washington as the leader of the Constitutional Convention. For many of the delegates, Washington was a symbol of dignity, stability, authority, and restraint. They wanted a government that was very much like Washington, strong but protective of the rights of the people. His presence at the convention was essential. With his leadership the delegates were able to come together, put aside their differences, and create a government for the good of the people.

James Madison: "The Father of the Constitution"

James Madison of Virginia contributed greatly to the Constitution. Like George Washington, Madison believed in a strong central government. He came to the convention with a unique plan for the nation. He had worked out this plan with the help of the other Virginia delegates. It was called the Virginia Plan.

Madison's plan involved throwing out the Articles of Confederation and establishing a different kind of government. Under the Articles of Confederation, Congress was unicameral, which means it had only one house. The Virginia Plan featured a legislature that would be bicameral, or having two houses.

This is the first page of James Madison's Virginia Plan, which became, in large part, the basis for the United States Constitution.

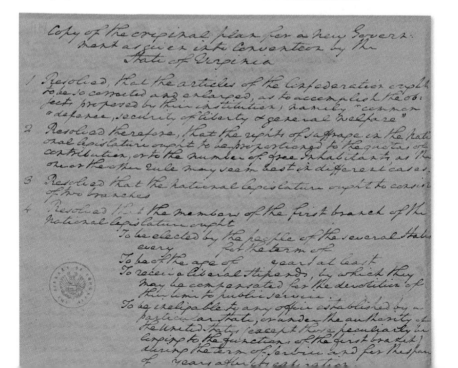

Madison's plan also called for three branches of government, none of which were allowed to become too powerful. It supported the idea of a strong national government to hold the states together.

The delegates rejected many of the details of Madison's Virginia Plan, but in the end, his key ideas were included in the Constitution. The Constitution created a republic with three branches of government and a system of checks and balances to keep each branch from becoming too strong.

Madison was one of the most regular speakers at the convention. His Virginia Plan was very influential. Madison also contributed to

James Madison is called "The Father of the Constitution."

the wording of the Constitution and kept thorough notes on the debates that took place. Madison was exceptionally active in the making of the Constitution.

Benjamin Franklin believed in a strong national government.

Benjamin Franklin: "The Sage of the Constitutional Convention"

A *sage* is a wise person who is honored for his or her experience and judgment. Benjamin Franklin, a delegate from Pennsylvania, was called "The Sage of the Constitutional Convention."

Like Washington and Madison, Franklin believed that the country needed a strong central government. At the age of eighty-one, he was the oldest delegate to the convention. He contributed his wisdom and his experience to the framing of the new Constitution.

In his lifetime, Franklin was a writer, a scientist, an inventor, an ambassador, and a political leader. He had great curiosity, an adventurous spirit, and a love of knowledge. The delegates respected him, and he was often able to soothe their tempers when arguments broke out. Franklin knew the wisdom of compromise.

Franklin was not happy about everything in the final Constitution, but he signed the document anyway. In his own words, "I expect no better because I am not sure, that it is not the best." He encouraged other delegates who did not like the Constitution to sign it. He knew that it would not be easy to build the government that they had designed on paper, but he also believed that nothing was more worth trying for.

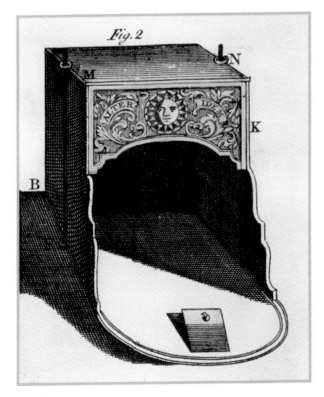

In addition to his other occupations, Benjamin Franklin was an inventor. Some of his many inventions include the lightning rod, the Franklin stove, and bifocal glasses.

Alexander Hamilton:
"The Champion of the Constitution"

New York delegate Alexander Hamilton believed that the United States needed a stronger central government. However, Hamilton's ideas were more extreme than those of most of the other delegates.

Hamilton believed that senators and the leader of the executive branch should serve for life. He also thought that state governments were unnecessary, and that all power should be given to the central government. Most of the delegates disagreed with Hamilton's ideas. They felt that the strong government Hamilton wanted was too similar to the tyrannous government of Britain.

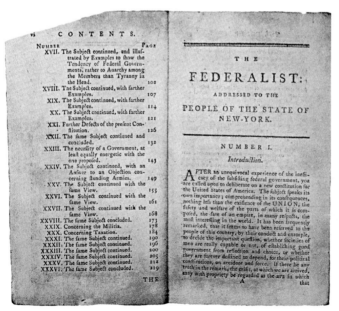

Alexander Hamilton, James Madison, and John Jay wrote a collection of essays called *The Federalist* in support of the Constitution.

Alexander Hamilton wanted a strong central government.

Hamilton was not completely happy with the Constitution. He was afraid that the new government would be too weak to last. However, he knew the importance of compromise, and he knew that the Constitution was better than the Articles of Confederation. He put his own opinions aside and signed the document.

Hamilton did not stop there. He wrote essays encouraging the states to **ratify** the Constitution. He spoke out in support of the document. One after another, the states agreed to ratify it. With the help of leaders like Alexander Hamilton, people who were brave enough to put their own opinions aside, the Constitution became law.

George Mason proposal to include a bill of rights in the Constitution was defeated.

Other Voices

Washington, Madison, Franklin, and Hamilton were all in favor of a strong national government. However, there were plenty of delegates at the Constitutional Convention who were not. George Mason, another Virginia delegate, was one of them.

Mason voiced concern that a strong government would lead to a President who was like a king. He worried that the central government would have too much power over the states. He also worried that a strong government would not protect the rights of the people, such as freedom of the press and freedom of religion.

Mason was not the only person who spoke out for the rights of the people. Thomas Jefferson was not a delegate to the Constitutional Convention. He was in Europe, serving as the American Minister to France. However, Jefferson made it known that while he was in favor of a strong government, he also believed that the Constitution needed a bill of rights. In fact, many delegates and many citizens across the nation voiced concern about this. Mercy Otis Warren, a writer from Massachusetts, wrote a criticism of the Constitution. One of her main complaints was that it contained no bill of rights.

So many people wanted a bill of rights that most state governments insisted, as a condition of ratification, that the first Congress add a bill of rights that would guarantee freedom of religion, freedom of speech, freedom of the press, and a number of other basic freedoms.

Mercy Otis Warren supported individual rights.

Another important voice belonged to Roger Sherman from Connecticut. Sherman came up with one of the most important compromises in the Constitution.

Many delegates disagreed about the number of representatives each state should have in Congress. The larger states thought that the number should be based on population. This meant that Virginia, for example, would have more representatives than Delaware.

Roger Sherman came up with the Great Compromise.

However, the smaller states were afraid of losing what little power they had. They insisted that every state have the same number of representatives, regardless of population.

Roger Sherman came up with a solution. He suggested that Congress should have two houses. The number of members in one house of Congress should depend on state population, while the number of members in the other house should be the same for every state. After much debate the delegates agreed. The agreement became known as the Great Compromise. Because of Roger Sherman's suggestion, the delegates were able to proceed with their task of creating the Constitution.

Cooperation and Compromise

On September 17, 1787, thirty-nine of the fifty-five delegates to the Constitutional Convention signed the Constitution. Some of the delegates, such as George Washington and Benjamin Franklin, were among the most famous people in the country. Others, such as Roger Sherman, were less well-known people whose contributions were equally important. For the signers of the Constitution, the document was a triumph of cooperation and compromise. Almost all of them had concerns about the Constitution, but they were determined to create the greatest government they could. They knew that the Constitution was the very best they could do and hoped that it would build a strong and free nation.

By late summer of 1788, the Constitution had been ratified by eleven states and became law. Slowly, our country formed and grew around its Constitution.

The Constitution that worked for our young nation long ago still works today. For this accomplishment we must thank the leaders of the Constitutional Convention who came together in the spirit of strength, liberty, cooperation, and compromise.

The United States Constitution was signed on September 17, 1787.

Glossary

checks and balances a system in which each branch of government checks the power of the other branches

compromise a deal in which each side gives up something in order to reach an agreement

delegate a representative

executive branch the part of the government that is in charge of enforcing our nation's laws

judicial branch the part of the government that is in charge of interpreting our nation's laws

legislative branch the part of the government that makes our nation's laws

ratify to approve